VISUAL THINKING STRATEGIES IN
Montessori
ENVIRONMENTS

National Center for Montessori in the Public Sector
and Philip Yenawine

NATIONAL CENTER for
MONTESSORI in the PUBLIC SECTOR

VISUAL THINKING STRATEGIES IN MONTESSORI ENVIRONMENTS
National Center for Montessori in the Public Sector and Philip Yenawine

Copyright © 2022 by National Center for Montessori in the Public Sector

All rights reserved.

Published in the United States by National Center for Montessori in the Public Sector Press

Visit our web site at public-montessori.org

Library of Congress Control Number: 2021923466

ISBN Paperback: 978-1-7338691-2-6
ISBN Kindle: 978-1-7338691-3-3
ISBN ePub: 978-1-7338691-4-0

Printed in the United States of America

Book design by Danielle Foster
Cover design by Danielle Foster
Cover art The Hill of the Favela by Tarsila do Amaral

First Paperback Edition

*With love, we dedicate this playbook to Jacqueline Cossentino,
vibrant and tireless champion of Montessori,
whose life and work were tragically cut short
just as the book was being completed.*

Foreword

The National Center for Montessori in the Public Sector (NCMPS) has been a proponent of Visual Thinking Strategies (VTS) since our inception, and we thank Jackie Cossentino, co-founder of NCMPS, for bringing VTS to our work.

Jackie began her career in museum education. Through her museum work, Jackie found VTS and began building what would be a long and rich professional relationship with Philip Yenawine, author, master museum teacher, Montessori grandparent, and co-founder of VTS. Through VTS, Jackie found Montessori and went on to be a Montessori parent, school administrator, researcher, and co-founder of NCMPS.

Jackie and Philip worked together as VTS colleagues, fellow travelers in the education reform world, and writing partners. They shared the hope that Montessori practitioners could gain a deeper understanding of both the theoretical congruences between VTS and Montessori and the practical applications that can be implemented in the classroom and beyond.

We at NCMPS are grateful to Jackie and Philip for their groundbreaking work. We are honored and eager to share this work with the Montessori community and to carry on their tradition of training teachers in a technique that brings joy, aesthetic wisdom, logic, and literacy to all who partake.

Contents

CHAPTER 1 **VTS and Montessori** 1

Why a Playbook and How to Use It 2
VTS and Montessori 3
Following the Viewer 5
Looking, Thinking & Talking: The Social Life of Critical Thinking 6
    Visual Thinking and the First Plane Child 9
    Visual Thinking and the Second Plane Child 11
    Visual Thinking and the Third Plane Child 12
Further Reading 14

CHAPTER 2 **Getting Started with VTS** 15

Basic Guidelines for Facilitating VTS Lessons 17
    Choosing pictures: the subject of the discussion 17
    Starting the lesson 17
    Asking the questions 18
    Responding to students' comments 18
    Concluding the lesson 19

Here's what you might expect to happen in a lower elementary class	19
More notes on choosing pictures	21
Making Thinking Visible: The Art of Paraphrase	21
Conditional phrasing samples	23
Basic Orienting Vocabulary	25
Terms and Phrases to Avoid	26
VTS and the Prepared Environment	26
The Museum Visit	28
Further Reading	29

CHAPTER 3   ## VTS and Language Development   31

Early Childhood: Curiosity, Fluency, and Language Explosions	32
VTS and Emerging Vocabulary	35
Childhood and Adolescence: Conceptual and Social Exploration	36
Building on Skills Developed through Looking and Discussing	38
Looking Circles	39
Building Skills through Writing and Research	40
Informal Writing	40
Research and Other Formal Writing	42
Further Reading	43

CHAPTER 4   ## VTS and Assessment   **45**

Looking, Thinking, and Talking . . . and Growing   47

Measuring Thinking   49

    What Growth Looks Like: Applying VTS Research Methodology   49

Abstracting the Method: Tools for Assessing Discussion and Writing   51

    Pre- and Post-Writing Samples   54

Writing Examples Discussed   55

Assessing Writing   61

Counting What Counts   63

Further Reading   64

CHAPTER 5   ## Further Reflections   **65**

Cosmic Education, Human Potential, and Aesthetic Development   66

    Imagination Is Grounded in Perception   68

Acknowledgments   **70**

CHAPTER 1

VTS and Montessori

This playbook is written for adults who are working with children in Montessori learning environments. Drawing from nearly three decades of research on Visual Thinking Strategies (VTS), aesthetic development, and critical thinking, combined with a growing body of work on human development, deep literacy, and transformational educational initiatives, this book will equip you—the Montessori educator—to make the most of VTS within the Montessori context.

Why a Playbook and How to Use It

Everyone who worked on this book has long, firsthand connections to Visual Thinking Strategies and to Montessori, both personally and professionally. We have seen VTS and Montessori function independently of one another and in tandem. And we have gained an appreciation of how the two pedagogies align in purpose and in practice, putting students at the center of learning and creating opportunities for them to engage in critical thinking, complex conversations, and meaningful collaborations.

We believe that VTS in a Montessori classroom can be a powerful additional tool that enhances aesthetic thought and cognitive growth of learners, young or old. Accordingly, the purpose of this Playbook is to assist Montessori practitioners in gaining both a deeper understanding of the theoretical convergences between VTS and Montessori and the practical applications that can be implemented in the classroom and beyond.

Many readers will have taken a VTS training, possibly even one focused specifically on Montessori learning environments. This book serves as a companion to those experiences. Chapter 2, for instance, presents the 'how' of a VTS discussion. However, just as this book cannot replace Montessori training, it is not meant to supplant the experience of learning to be a VTS facilitator. It can, however, reinforce concepts and skills explored during training. In Chapter 3, we delve more deeply into the convergences between VTS and the development of language skills at each plane of development. We include discussions of the why of language explosions, conceptual and social exploration, and concrete examples of materials you may prepare and activities that are pitched for particular classroom environments. Chapter 4 addresses VTS and data: how you can direct observation toward tracking and assessing what children are learning through VTS. Chapter 5 reflects on the wider linkages and meanings of aesthetic development and human potential.

Chapter 1: VTS and Montessori

WILLIAM H. JOHNSON, SOAPBOX RACING, SMITHSONIAN AMERICAN ART MUSEUM

VTS and Montessori

The mission of VTS is broad and ambitious—to transform education, especially for vulnerable students. Through facilitated discussions of carefully selected works of art, learners of all ages experience the thrill of discovering, communicating, and evaluating some of the deepest, most complex and enduring ideas humans have ever tried to express. Because works of visual art are accessible to anyone who is able to see, everyone—regardless of educational background, culture, ethnicity, or social class—can participate in rigorous and engaging inquiry. And the more we participate, the better we get at looking, thinking, and communicating our ideas.

Chapter 1: VTS and Montessori

Montessori educators understand that making, expressing, and experiencing meaning through art is a fundamental human need. And in most Montessori classrooms, art is included as a part of the study of culture and language. For very young children, experiences with visual art may revolve around discussions of pictures and objects that may be part of the prepared environment. For older students, the focus of lessons is more often on making or appreciating art. In the process, discussions of how and why art is made often ensue.

© AUBREY GEE / CHESAPEAKE MONTESSORI SCHOOL

VTS builds on the assumption that art is necessary and takes these discussions even further. Despite the fact that every culture at every time and in every place has made and appreciated art, too many people today (young as well as old) find themselves shut out of what art has to offer. Where most art in its original form was participatory—as part of religious ritual or social activity or cultural celebration—museums (the storehouses of visual art in our culture) have disconnected art from its origins and sequestered it in showcases most comfortable for people of relative privilege. VTS was developed to tear down the barriers that result and to move the experience of interacting with art back to the center of social life.

Following the Viewer

VTS is the brainchild of two US educators, a cognitive psychologist and a museum educator, whose shared experience told them that appreciating visual art has much more to do with learning how to look at it than with listening to how others explain it.

In 1988, art educator Philip Yenawine commissioned psychologist Abigail Housen to evaluate his education programs at the Museum of Modern Art in New York. Yenawine wanted to know what, if anything, visitors were learning when they participated in the museum's programs. Housen, similarly, wanted to know more about how people made sense of what they saw and heard, the same interest that had motivated her graduate studies.

The results of those initial studies were astounding. Despite asking for and taking advantage of museum education devices such as gallery talks, teacher workshops, extended courses, labels, and brochures, the vast majority of visitors, Housen concluded, took almost nothing away from such educational tools. For example, after a gallery talk, most listeners can't retrace their steps and remember what they saw; nor can they accurately recall what was said to them. Further, Housen found, the reason so little sticks with these visitors is that most museum education programs miss the mark: they tend to teach the content rather than the viewer. VTS was developed to change this tendency and make the education programs more meaningful.

Gestalt psychologist Rudolf Arnheim (1902-2007) coined the term "visual thinking" and argued that perception was so central to cognition that there is, functionally, no difference between looking and thinking.

> *Perception makes it possible to structure reality, and thus to attain knowledge. Art is a means of perception, a means of cognition... Art reveals to us the essence of things, the essence of our existence. That is its function.*[1]

---

1 Arnheim interview, 2001, http://www.cabinetmagazine.org/issues/2/rudolfarnheim.php.

Looking, in other words, shapes thinking. Art—a universal means of constructing meaning—expresses our deepest thoughts and feelings. Looking at and thinking about what we see in art enables us to organize thoughts and feelings in ways that shape our understandings of complex subjects. These understandings precede and inform language.

Visual Thinking Strategies takes its name from Arnheim's work. VTS co-founder Abigail Housen grounded her own theory of aesthetic development in Arnheim's psychological and philosophical ideas but went further. Where Arnheim was interested in describing a process of viewing, Housen wanted to learn how viewing manifested in the ways people make sense of art. More specifically, she wanted to know what people think about when they look at art, and what, if anything, causes people to grow as art viewers.

What she learned was that aesthetic development is both intricately linked to human development in general and somewhat separate as a process. That is, like general human development, which takes place in phases or planes, aesthetic development also occurs in successive stages. Those stages, however, are not linked to chronological age or even education level. Rather, they are the result of a viewer's experience with looking at and thinking about art.

Using Housen's data about how people think at the early stages of experience, VTS is designed for the skills, interests, and needs of beginning viewers. Its aim is to nurture but not necessarily hasten stage change; each stage is necessary and valuable on its own terms. Rather, the goal is to enable viewers to experience their stage fully and to cultivate the qualities of aesthetic thinking that allow us to contemplate and express the deepest meanings of our existence—something within reach of people even early in their experience with art if drawn into it in authentic, stage-appropriate ways.

Looking, Thinking & Talking: The Social Life of Critical Thinking

One of the things that makes VTS different from other types of discussion or discovery-based learning is the immediate nature of the thinking process stimulated by images. Unlike linguistic texts, which are comprehended through a complex process of linear decoding, pictures are captured as whole impressions, triggering associations and feelings, often simultaneously. It is, in fact, the presence of emotion connected to ideas or memories that makes the experience of looking at art so compelling. This linking of thought and feeling—what Housen has called "thoughtful feelings" or "feelingful thoughts"—is one way we distinguish aesthetic thought from other types of cognitive activity.

We all engage in aesthetic thought, but our thoughts become more complex and more sophisticated with experience. And research has shown that when aesthetic thinking happens in a group, growth both accelerates and becomes more robust. Learning to think, in other words, is a social activity. Figure 1.1, developed by Harry Lasker, formerly on the faculty of Harvard Graduate School of Education, traces the interactive nature of cognitive and social activity that takes place during a VTS discussion.

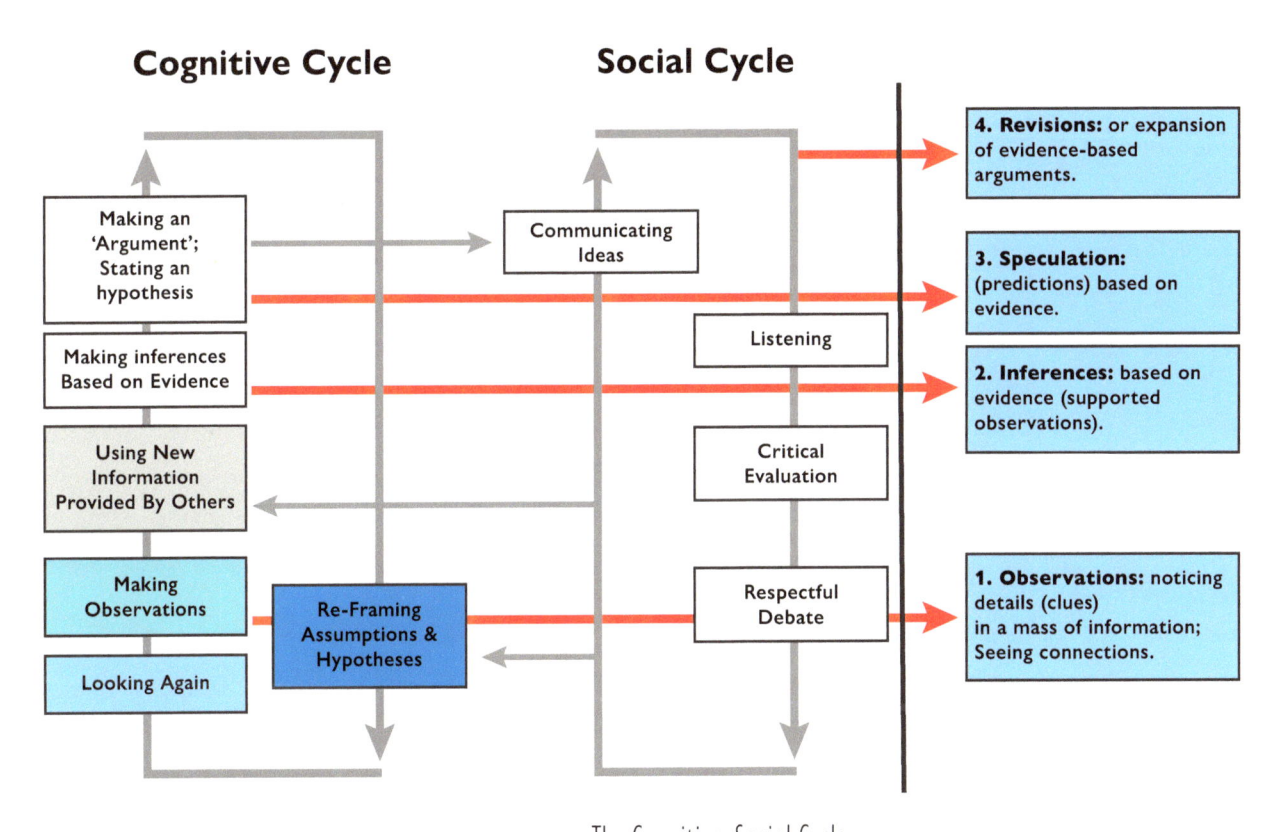

FIGURE 1.1 The Cognitive, Social Cycle

The process begins with silent observation. Guided by three essential questions, observations are then shared. A first comment might be called an individual's opening interpretation: for example, "I see a girl who is sad." As soon as that interpretation is spoken, it becomes part of the group process. Subsequent commenters might agree or disagree with the opening statement: "I think she looks more serious than sad." They might identify other details: "A storm is coming." Or relay a personal association: "She looks like my little cousin."

Each time a comment is entered into the discussion, the facilitator paraphrases it, which has the dual effect of slowing down the pace of the discussion (providing what Philip Yenawine calls "noodling time") and validating each comment as an element of the collaborative meaning making the group is engaged in. The facilitator also links comments showing how each interacts with prior observations and constitutes a piece of the structure, or scaffold, the group collectively builds as ideas are articulated, affirmed, debated, and re-framed. (The elements of VTS are described in detail in Chapter 2.)

Since children's ideas often out stretch their available language, accurate paraphrasing also models syntax and vocabulary needed to clarify and reinforce what's been said and assists others in understanding the meanings all are searching for.

When students feel safe to offer observations and the facilitator paraphrases every comment with accuracy, the thinking of individuals as well as the collective is made visible. The result offers a window not only into what viewers think about what they see, but also how they think.

Over time, viewers get better at this collective building of meaning. Because of both experience and skilled facilitation, observations become more precise, comments are increasingly grounded in evidence from the picture, and alternative interpretations are proposed, considered, and factored into an ongoing iterative process.

The process is organic, driven by the viewers themselves with the facilitator serving as witness to, clarifier of, and protector of the process. For teachers, the spare and predictable nature of the VTS script enables the facilitator to liberate herself from the obligation to impart knowledge. Knowing the questions that propel the discussion allows a sharp focus on listening to what students are saying about what they see. The simple, repeated pattern of the method allows students to learn and habitually employ a means to shape what they learn, something they instinctively apply to many contexts as part of learning how to learn. Both teachers and students often find themselves asking the VTS questions, especially the one that asks for evidence, again and again.

Chapter 1: VTS and Montessori

Visual Thinking and the First Plane Child

For children between the ages of three and six, VTS is most obviously linked to sense training and language development. Visual perception is both a necessary prerequisite for and an aide to language development. Montessori educators consider the 3-6 prepared environment a living laboratory for language; the space is intentionally designed to provide hundreds of objects to discover, name, and incorporate into conversation. And the progression toward reading begins with conversation, progresses first to writing, and finally to reading. The "sensorial" exercises, most obviously linked to later work in mathematics and geometry, also provide the child generous practice in the development of visual discrimination with two and three-dimensional objects. This practice is enhanced by structured experiences of art.

Chapter 1: VTS and Montessori

PICASSO, PABLO. LE GOURMET. 1901. OIL ON CANVAS. 36 9/16" × 26 7/8". NATIONAL GALLERY OF ART, CHESTER DALE COLLECTION: WASHINGTON, DC.

In early childhood, VTS resonates most effectively as an opportunity to identify and name. The most appropriate images for this age group are those that contain many identifiable figures (children, other people, animals), activities and interactions (eating, sleeping, reading, playing games), familiar objects (grass, stones, mountains, a church, a house). And while it's most common for children at this age to list what they see, some children also begin to tell stories.

As the period of most rapid brain development, the first plane is also a period of intensive development of executive functions. The key skills of working memory, inhibition, and cognitive flexibility are necessary for self-regulation as well as intellectual growth. And just as the prepared environment is exquisitely designed to support the acquisition and refinement of these skills, VTS during this period gives children valuable practice in speculation, considering multiple points of view, and self-control.

Visual Thinking and the Second Plane Child

As children between the ages of six and twelve become increasingly fluent readers, their ability and interest in research and inquiry grows accordingly. As "conceptual explorers," elementary children demonstrate an almost insatiable curiosity and a desire to ask and answer "why" as opposed to "what" questions. Likewise, the focus on naming objects shifts toward finding and telling stories about what is going on the pictures they see.

Within this context, the VTS question "What do you see that makes you say that?" becomes the centerpiece of group consideration of images. The request for evidence embedded in this question is experienced as a relevant and immediate challenge, one that can be undertaken collaboratively, and that can produce many satisfying answers. Within this context, the skills of affirming, differing, reasoning, and speculating are developed alongside inferring, fluent storytelling, and respectful debating.

Moreover, as children become more adept at interpreting visual images, their questions begin to change. An interest in where and when the action is taking place, why an image looks like it does, and how the artist figures in surface over time, providing opportunities for authentic, interdisciplinary research. Likewise, the growing appreciation of art as a universal human tendency and a fundamental human need can both power and illustrate the integrated nature of Cosmic Education.

Visual Thinking and the Third Plane Child

Since the mid 1990s, developmental psychologists have studied the impact of VTS on elementary classrooms, and the outcomes have been remarkable. A summary of the research is available on the VTS website (www.vtshome.org).

More recently, new research on brain development, executive function, and the social/emotional needs of students between the ages of 11 and 18 suggest that the expressive, sensorial, and communal elements of the VTS experience may provide an especially potent environment in which to engage adolescent learners. We know that as adolescents experience significant physiological changes, they also grow increasingly social, emotionally volatile, and interested in novelty. Adolescents thrive when they have ample opportunities to work in groups, explore new topics, and contemplate complex ideas, especially those related to their own identity, power, social interactions, and future.

VTS lessons offer an authentic environment in which to give students access to deep, personal, and novel ideas. The images that stimulate VTS discussions are selected to address themes, concepts, and questions that are of interest to students regardless of age, but it turns out that piquing the interest and addressing the concerns, individual and collective, of adolescents is particularly germane. Getting and sustaining their attention requires skillful selecting of image topics and complexity. Images must address interactions and dilemmas students want to think about and come to terms with. Whether the medium is visual art, literature, social studies, or science, material that is accessible, open to multiple interpretations, and structured to provide an appropriate balance of accessibility and challenge is a crucial ingredient in ensuring successful learning. Challenging students is necessary particularly in the Third Plane.

In the next chapter we delve more deeply into the "how" of preparing for and facilitating a VTS discussion.

Further Reading

Arnheim, Rudolf. (1972). *Toward a Psychology of Art.* Berkeley and Los Angeles: University of California Press.

Bruner, Jerome. (1989). *Thoughts on Art Education.* Brentwood, CA: Getty Center for Education in the Arts.

Vygotsky, Lev. (1962). *Thought and Language.* Cambridge, MA: MIT Press.

Vygotsky, Lev. (1978). *Mind in Society.* Cambridge, MA: Harvard University Press.

Yenawine, Philip. (2018). *Visual Thinking Strategies for Preschool: Using Art to Enhance Language and Social Skills.* Cambridge: Harvard Education Press.

Yenawine, Philip. (2013). *Visual Thinking Strategies: Using Art to Deepen Learning Across Schools Disciplines.* Cambridge: Harvard Education Press.

CHAPTER 2

Getting Started with VTS

Understanding the theoretical convergences between Montessori and VTS is a good start to integrating the practice into your classroom. But it is only a start. In this chapter, we address the "how" of VTS pedagogy. We begin with an overview of the process of facilitating VTS discussions, which will be a review for some of our readers. But to make sure we are all clear about what's involved in VTS teaching, we spell out the details.

Chapter 2: Getting Started with VTS

Although it's possible that a practiced Montessori teacher will pick up VTS facilitation based on reading about it, it's not expected. Training has proved useful to most of us and is available from two sources: online from www.watershed-ed.org and www.public-montessori.org or in person from www.vtshome.org. After the details of VTS facilitation are articulated, we then move on to address how Montessori teachers often choose to incorporate VTS into the prepared environment.

EDWARD HOPPER, CAPE COD MORNING, 1950 SMITHSONIAN AMERICAN ART MUSEUM

Basic Guidelines for Facilitating VTS Lessons

Choosing pictures: the subject of the discussion

Present a carefully selected image, one that provokes good discussion. Productive choices contain:

- Subjects of interest to your students: images that are immediately engaging.

- Some familiar depiction given students' existing knowledge, taking into account what you know of their varied life experiences. Recognizable imagery gives students places to start; opening comments become reference points for the rest of the discussion.

- Storylines/narratives also with accessible meaning, again thinking about your specific students. Puzzling them piques interest and motivates ideas; confounding them discourages them instead.

- Ambiguity and multiple possible meanings: room for probing, for differing interpretations and changes of mind.

- Diversity of visual language, medium, and maker, encouraging flexibility.

Starting the lesson

- Introduce VTS if they're new to it. For example, tell them it allows them to examine art, to think, to contribute observations and ideas, to listen, and to build understandings together. Later in the term and depending on their age, you might ask students what they think they learn from VTS.

- Project the image you've chosen and ask the students to study it for a moment in silence before you invite them to speak. For very young people, make the looking a task with specific directions: for example, look from top to bottom, side to side, look for big details and small ones.

Asking the questions

- After they have examined the image, ask the question, **"What's going on (or what's happening) in this picture?"** For three- and four-year-olds, start with: What do you see in this picture? Or what do you notice? For older students and for young ones as soon as you think they are ready, use the "what's going on" wording. Ask this question only once to get the discussion started.

- Whenever students make a comment that involves an inference drawn from observations, respond first by paraphrasing (see below,) and then ask, **"What do you see that makes you say that?"** After a few lessons, some students will provide evidence without prompting. Listen for this; they have learned the behavior prompted by the question, and it means that you don't need to (and shouldn't) repeat the question. Instead acknowledge the evidence in your paraphrase.

- In order to keep students searching for further observations, before each new person comments, ask, **"What more can we find?"** With young children you might phrase the question, "What more do you notice?" Even with their hands in the air, ask the question. You want to keep positing the idea that there's always more to be found or thought about, great training for discussions of many topics.

Responding to students' comments

- **Listen carefully** to catch everything a person says. If very young children (or second language learners) see something but struggle for words, let them come to the image and point. If you can't find what someone sees, ask for help: "Can you show us what you're seeing?" If you don't understand what they mean, also ask for help: "Can you add more words to help us understand?"

- **Point to what they mention** in the image—a visual paraphrase—and pinpoint again as you paraphrase. Be precise. Point to what is mentioned even if the element has been mentioned before; you are acknowledging each student.

- **Paraphrase each comment**, no matter how short, taking a moment to reflect if you need to. Show you understand the student's meaning. In rephrasing, change the wording, but not the meaning of what is said. Model proper sentence construction and rich vocabulary to assist students with language. Use conditional verbs ("could be" or "might be," for example) to convey that interpretations are not facts ("correct") but possibilities.

- **Accept each comment neutrally** by treating everyone and each comment the same way. Remember that this process emphasizes a useful pattern of thinking, not right answers. Students are learning to make detailed observations, sorting out and applying what they know to make sense of something at least partially unfamiliar. Thinking itself and articulating their thoughts leads to growth even when students see and think things you don't.

- **Link answers that relate** whether people agree, disagree, or build on one another's ideas. Show how the students' thinking evolves, how some observations and ideas stimulate others, and how opinions change and build.

Concluding the lesson

Thank students for their participation. Avoid summaries; linking throughout is enough to show how conversations build. Instead, tell them what you particularly enjoyed or appreciated. Suggest that they might have more ideas as they reflect on the image and discussion. Also allow them to share ideas they didn't get to contribute with people sitting next to them.

Here's what you might expect to happen in a lower elementary class

Let's say you've already had a few VTS discussions with your lower elementary students. First thing one morning, you assemble the class and comfortably situate them so that all can easily see. You project your chosen image, or for example, the image on the next page, asking the students to study it in silence for a few moments, then start the discussion with the opening question: "What's going on in this picture?"

You might expect the first comment to include much of what's depicted, pointing out that some people are sitting around a table in an old-fashioned room. After paraphrasing and pointing your finger to take in everything the child mentioned, you would probably ask: "What do you see that makes you say 'old-fashioned?'"

You would paraphrase the evidence provided and then, even with many hands in the air, would ask, "What more can we find?"

The next comment might mention the child with her back to us, her head on her father's knee. Additional comments might lead us to the action of the female figure or the identity of the gentleman in black. Over time details such as his umbrella and top hat might be mentioned. The cat might come up next, and maybe the banjo—perhaps a thought about it being used to entertain the person who seems to be a guest. The other two children will likely figure in at some point, leading to the discovery of the suspicious look the one casts toward the visitor. The condition of the father's clothes and maybe the mother's apron might elicit comments. At some point along the way it's likely to come up that the people are Black. The paraphrasing and linking will help build the idea that the many observations and inferences drawn add up to a story about a family together, maybe having a meal, with a well-dressed visitor.

A solid fifteen minutes passes, and it's time to move onto the next image—you have planned two or three for this session. You thank the students for noticing so much in the picture and for contributing ideas to an unfolding story you found interesting. You might let them partner-share ideas you didn't have time to hear.

More notes on choosing pictures

VTS image discussions require a picture chosen for your students. We hope it's clear from the one above what makes a piece of art work: some information that is easy to recognize and talk about, some elements that take time to find, and others that provoke some wondering. The image should present a story that can be pieced together as many comments are made, discoveries are shared, and observations and ideas are discussed.

Both www.vtshome.org and www.watershed-ed.org have compendiums of tested images available for teachers, and the prepared environment supplies more. The internet makes it very easy to find additional images to tailor choices to your students and your teaching goals at a particular moment. In using VTS, we suggest you steer away from images that are dense, abstract, murky, or macabre. It's not that children cannot deal with these in some ways, but we recommend giving them images that allow them to compute meanings that add to their trove of memories in positive ways. Nudes should be avoided as well, out of respect for the values of children's home environments and cultures. There is enough time later for the broader range of options our very visual world produces.

Making Thinking Visible: The Art of Paraphrase

VTS facilitation is designed to ensure a student-centered learning process. Students' ideas drive the conversation; their observations and ideas are the content of the discussion. All aspects of the method support this objective. The questions activate the students' open-ended thinking. Listening enables you to take in, consider, and respond to what each child says. Pointing ensures that you and everyone else sees what's mentioned. Paraphrasing makes sure everyone hears each idea validated by your rephrasing, encouraging students also to value each idea. Linking demonstrates how their thoughts interact.

Through the process of looking, thinking, and discussing an image, students are trying to understand what is depicted and what it means to them. They are constructing meaning together. Each comment, and your paraphrase of it, constitutes a block in the students' construction of meaning. One way of understanding how this leads to learning is to think of a scaffold, a term developmental psychologist Lev Vygotsky applied to capture the social and constructive way in which humans build knowledge together. We scaffold on each other's existing knowledge and ideas to come to new understandings ourselves.

Teachers facilitate this scaffolding during VTS discussions, creating an environment for meaningful participation that leads to learning. The facilitator's task is to ensure that all observations and ideas are welcomed, treating students equally and giving all comments equal emphasis. Pointing to what is mentioned as you listen starts this. Skillful paraphrasing further reinforces the fact that each idea matters to you and to the discussion. Through intentional rephrasing of the observations and ideas students offer, you provide the foundational elements of the scaffold.

As comments accumulate, you can begin to hear how they respond to one another— how the scaffold builds observation by observation. Linking comments points out to students that this is happening. Linking cites the ways comments relate to one another—agreeing, disagreeing, adding to or building on, or bringing in something new. You might say, for example. "So, Michelle *agrees with* Malik that the man is probably a visitor and *she adds that* his clothes make him seem different from the others."

Paraphrasing requires choosing language carefully. Both the viewer and the rest of the group need to hear that you understand their thoughts, and you demonstrate this by putting their core meaning or meanings into your own words. The basic requirements for a useful paraphrase are that it be accurate, complete, and yet still succinct, making sure the ideas are expressed clearly and that they include the vocabulary students search for. Do not add to or alter the thinking: just change the words. If and when students supply evidence to back up an idea, make sure you include it: "You think the boy might be suspicious of the visitor because of the way he's looking at him."

The sample paraphrases above introduce another element of skillful paraphrasing: using conditional or qualifying language as you rephrase. For example, use verbs that suggest possibility instead of certainty. So, you can say "she *might be* crying" or "you're suggesting that *maybe* most of these people aren't very happy" or "so you think the little girl *could be* sad or *maybe* just shy." Very young children often don't like this "could be" phrasing because of the very concrete way their minds work and, consequently, they may hold on to their ideas firmly. Try it anyway because soon they need to know that, legitimate as one's ideas and opinions are, most are subjective even when backed up with evidence.

Rephrasing comments conditionally helps build the consciousness that, while it's great to have and express one's thoughts, they should be considered alongside the valid ideas and opinions of others—not as truths, necessarily, but possibilities. As result, one element documented in VTS research is that students build the capacity to consider various alternative opinions as plausible, which we consider a hallmark of both visual literacy and critical thinking. Art objects as topics support this growth: They are naturally ambiguous and layered and leaving their meanings open-ended is appropriate.

Conditional phrasing samples

Instead of "Suzy sees a family," try "Suzy sees a group of people in this picture and thinks they might be a family." Or **"Suzy is noticing what could be a family."**

Instead of "The mother is serving food," try "Marco notices this figure (pointing at her) and think it's the mom who might be putting food on the man's plate."

Instead of "Carol notices these two other boys," try "Carol notices these other two figures and wonders if they could be boys."

A final element designed to help students understand the meanings they construct as they discuss the images is "framing." The ability to frame the thoughts usually develops after extensive practice. Here's an example: In the introduction to a paraphrase, the facilitator might say, "So you are *thinking about the historical era shown in this picture* and you think it was maybe a hundred years ago. Your evidence is the furniture and the fireplace." The teacher points out to the student that she is using the framework of history as she thinks about what she sees. This enables the group to hear and appreciate not only "what" meanings are being ascribed to the picture but also "how" those meanings are being constructed—different thinking behaviors that together make meaningful sense of the image. As the facilitator steps back from simply paying attention to what is said and adds what kind of cognition it represents, the students gain yet another insight into what it means to construct one's understanding of previously unfamiliar material.

Below are some examples of phrasing that frames the kinds of thinking students use during discussions as well as how to link ideas that relate.

Framing simple comments: the vocabulary you can use to frame straightforward observations.

Emilia sees a tree.

John is noticing these three figures.

Kim is drawing our attention to… another part of the picture… or another detail… or this object.

Framing other types of thinking: a sampling of ways to frame thinking students use once they've moved beyond simple observations—associating, remembering, applying existing information, agreeing/disagreeing, wondering, puzzling, finding a narrative, speculating about possibilities, considering the artist/maker, supplying evidence, elaborating on an earlier thought, and revising an understanding.

This is reminding Miguel of…

Maia is drawing on background knowledge and thinks…

Kelly is curious about…

Sally is finding a story about…

Cindy is thinking about the artists and focusing on…

<u>Framing as part of linking related comments:</u> pointing out both the thinking behavior you notice and how it evolves and scaffolds—how students refer to one another's ideas.

You are agreeing/disagreeing with Elsie that this could be a…

Del is building on what Kelly said about…

Three of you have mentioned how the picture is making you think about…

John Carlo is offering a theory that's a little different from Cindy's…

We now have three different ideas about what this picture might be about… (paraphrase)

Basic Orienting Vocabulary

IMAGE—Another word for picture. Facilitation of image discussions doesn't require art knowledge. Because our primary aim is to broaden the skills applied to looking, we tend to steer away from using technical terms like painting (it's often hard to tell what something is), portrait, or perspective, and so forth, unless students mention them or are searching for a precise word to categorize what they see.

FIGURE—Any living being depicted in the picture. The gender of a person or the identity of an animal might be ambiguous, therefore subject to legitimate debate, and differences of opinion often lead to lively discussions.

OBJECT—Any nonliving thing a viewer might identify—boat, rake, backpack, broom. In many cases, an object that looks to be one thing (such as a factory) to one viewer might be seen as something else (perhaps a school) by another.

BACKGROUND—The part of the picture that appears to be farther away from the viewer—often it appears toward the top of the picture frame.

FOREGROUND—The part of the picture that appears to be closest to the viewer—often it appears near the bottom of the picture frame.

Terms and Phrases to Avoid

As you frame, avoid language that suggests fixed understanding. Words like "belief" imply a position that speakers often find themselves defending rather than exploring. Beliefs and some opinions, moreover, are not easily grounded in evidence; in some cases, beliefs may be so strong as to be immune from the persuasive power of evidence.

VTS and the Prepared Environment

Integrating VTS into your classroom may take many forms. It's most important to remember that within VTS, art images are tools for thinking and communicating. They are, therefore, extensions of your language and cultural areas, and can be prepared in ways similar to other language and cultural materials. Within the context of a VTS lesson, the image is the catalyst for group discussion. On their own, VTS images can serve as prompts for conversation between children or among children and adults, as well as for both formal and informal writing.

© AUBREY GEE / CHESAPEAKE MONTESSORI SCHOOL

Within the context of the formal VTS lesson, many Montessori teachers who integrate VTS into their environments invest in 8x10 color reproductions of images from the curriculum. They may be placed in frames in the language area or (for older students) collected in notebooks for student reference for either writing or research projects.

For children younger than five, we recommend offering VTS during the morning work period as a brief, small-group discussion to which anyone interested is invited. Beginning at age five, VTS lessons are whole-group events. Frequent discussions will further integrate VTS into the culture of your classroom. We recommend that students have a discussion weekly (in place of a late morning or early afternoon read-aloud is ideal).

VTS discussions work best using projected images, so everyone can see the image clearly and note details. Whether you are using a SmartBoard or an LCD projector, the classroom will need to be arranged so that all students can see the pictures and so that you can stand and point as students offer their comments. For classrooms that do not have access to SmartBoards, it is worth investing in a high-quality LCD projector.

VTS also works well in the context of distance learning with children as young as six. It's best if students have computers at home; tablets and phones are smaller and therefore seeing an image is harder, though they may be used in the absence of choice. The teacher uses a videoconferencing application (such as Zoom) that allows a group to form and a screen to be shared. If the group is larger than eight, it's useful to have two adults involved, one facilitating while the other acts as moderator, calling on students whose raised hands the facilitator can't see. The facilitator presents the chosen image in a slide show format, as large as possible. Images must be the highest resolution that can be found. You want students to easily find details, something that's actually easier online than in class. Pointing can be done with the cursor. If the intention is to have discussions of more than one image, it makes sense to put them into a presentation application such as PowerPoint, where it's easy to progress from one image to the next.

The Museum Visit

For older students (elementary and above), VTS is well suited to visiting a local museum, either as a structured field trip or as a student-planned "going out." Advance planning should include choosing images students will enjoy discussing.

Make sure that the museum is comfortable in letting you teach your own students. Also plan to give students time to work in small groups, pairs, or even alone, and check with the museum to make sure this is allowed. Writing projects are a great kind of assignment to give, especially if you let students choose the work they want to write about. Students might take a photo of the art object to accompany their writing, if the museum allows it, and most do. Purchasing postcards can be another way of bringing the visit back to school with you.

A "going out" that revolves around a museum visit could be stimulated by a desire for deeper investigation into a particular artist, era, or collection of art. Since these visits take place independent of the teacher (though with the support of a nonteaching adult), planning the visit is almost entirely the work of the students. Investigating the museum website for both logistical and content-based information is a usual first step. Determining how to get there, how long to stay, and how to navigate entrance, exploration, and return to school, are all part of the experience.

Further Reading

Yenawine, Philip. (2018). *Visual Thinking Strategies for Preschool: Using Art to Enhance Literacy and Social Skills.* Cambridge: Harvard Education Publishing Group.

Yenawine, Philip. (2013). *Visual Thinking Strategies: Using Art to Deepen Learning across Disciplines.* Cambridge: Harvard Education Publishing Group.

https://www.watershed-ed.org/

https://vtshome.org/

The New York Times Learning Network is an excellent source of images: https://www.nytimes.com/column/learning-whats-going-on-in-this-picture

CHAPTER 3

VTS and Language Development

Like everything in Montessori, language development is seen as a process that occurs in stages or planes. In this chapter, we move through the three school-age planes and discuss the ways in which VTS both converges with and enhances language development in Montessori classrooms.

Early Childhood: Curiosity, Fluency, and Language Explosions

Babies search their worlds with their eyes, and as they grow, their visual insights build. By the time they are three and four, they are adept at figuring out a great deal from looking around. In the best cases, parents, caregivers, and early childhood educators make use of this curiosity, desire to know, and visual acuity, to provide the basis for language and other learning. Playing on babies' incessant looking, the people around them who know to do so, name what a baby's gaze seems to rest on. They chat with the child about what happens and narrate activities connecting what is seen and experienced to words and sentences. Of course, they introduce illustrated books that captivate children's attention and provide a useful bridge from seeing to talking to reading

Both Montessori and VTS recognize that learning in general, and language development specifically, is grounded in sensory discrimination, especially visual acuity. Naming what babies see beginning in infancy primes language acquisition, and it is effective in that context because of its authenticity—it's real life. Letting babies talk about what they see and responding to their observations and thoughts—via dialogue—is invaluable in early childhood development, but a multifaceted approach to language development ongoing maintains the marriage among eye, mind, and language. The value of processing what we see through language doesn't end with schooling. We learn by looking and by way of language throughout life; they are partners.

In terms of the Montessori classroom, discussions of images of all kinds cement the connection between seeing (discovering, exploring) and oral language use—which comes before, and in turn enables, writing and reading. Large image banks also ultimately aid visualizing what is read, critical to comprehension.

As fluency increases, language becomes our principal cognitive tool, enabling us to both acquire and share knowledge, as well as to build and sustain relationships. As such, the ability to communicate through both oral and written language involves much more than the basic skills of phonemic awareness, vocabulary development or comprehension. Rather, the development of language and thought go hand in hand. Cognitive tools such as concentration and working memory foster language skills and vice versa. Language is also an emotional phenomenon. No one becomes a reader because they master reading strategies. Instead, deep literacy is inspired by desire to be part of a community—sometimes called "literate culture"—to discover new worlds, to connect with others, and to engage with challenging ideas. This is what Montessori meant when she described language "explosions."

Put another way, becoming authentically literate is an aesthetic experience. The catalyst for the experience is curiosity, and its fuel is fluency. Fluency refers to both the sound of speaking—smooth versus fragmented—and the capacity to translate thoughts into language. The ability to construct coherent strings of ideas and either speak or write them without a lot of attention to how one is doing it is one kind of fluent performance. Likewise, the ability to comprehend strings of ideas with ease while listening or reading is another. Becoming fluent happens through practice: lots of conversation, lots of writing, lots of reading, lots of thinking. In this way, fluency is both a means to, and an end of, language development.

What we talk, think, write, and read about matters. The more we care about a subject, the more likely we will be drawn to explore it alone and with others. The more we share our discoveries through language, the more fluent we become.

Language is a social activity grounded in culture. We "read" situations, facial expressions, and cultural norms. We feel connected—or alienated—when we recognize ourselves in our surroundings. This means that becoming fluent requires lots of opportunities to observe, experiment, and listen, as well as to name, interpret, and participate in conversation.

Moreover, learning environments that are truly "language rich" build from a foundation of order, calm, and beauty. They are filled with carefully selected items for children to name, manipulate, and consider. Adults use language intentionally, speaking with and not at children, enunciating words with care, and, generally focusing more on the quality rather than the quantity of spoken interaction. But the communication must be two way: children need to talk themselves, responding and offering ideas, and they need to hear each other talk for language to explode.

Many people, both within and beyond Montessori, emphasize the "phonics-based" nature of the curriculum. And while phonemic awareness is exemplified in materials such as sandpapers letters and the moveable alphabet, sound/symbol correspondence is only part of the sequence. Like the whole of the Montessori program, language development is an integrated enterprise. Because of an equal emphasis on choice and structure, the prepared environment is uniquely equipped to foster rigorous skill development grounded in genuine curiosity. Curiosity is a starting point for learning and the impetus for much of children's use of language.

Montessori called this spontaneous activity. To achieve spontaneous activity leading to language explosions, the child must have access to multiple modalities of engaging with language. During the course of a single morning, a three-year-old-child may tack back and forth between completing the surprisingly complex, multistep activity of washing a table, to a fetching game focused on retrieving successively longer rods ("bring me the longer one; bring me the longest one"), to a few minutes in the reading area perusing a picture book, with a break for authentic conversation with peers shared at a snack table. All this activity is self-chosen and none of it is aimless.

The point is that language is everywhere, and when the environment is carefully prepared for children who are absorbing language, everything in it is a potential teacher. This includes didactic materials as well as books, poetry, music, cultural artifacts, and art images.

VTS and Emerging Vocabulary

Language explosions are fueled by fluency and catalyzed by curiosity as well as vocabulary acquisition and usage. All of these are important elements in the process, particularly when it comes to oral communication. Words are tools for expressing oneself and very young children acquire these tools rapidly and, in a language-rich environment, seemingly effortlessly. Just as the prepared environment supplies myriad objects, people, and concepts, to identify, name, and manipulate, a well-chosen picture serves as a kind of virtual prepared environment, ready to meet viewers where they are.

Researchers at VTS have developed several collections of images for children beginning at age three. Those images have been chosen based, in part, on the variety of identifiable figures—balls, birds, cows, dogs, trees, flowers, houses, grass, clouds, clothes, and so on—children can name as they look at the pictures. Many of these words will fall into the frequently used category, often corresponding to actual objects seen in the classroom or in the home: pitchers, glasses, tables, chairs, spheres, toys, books, plants, and so on. Others will be less commonly used: shields, helmets, pastures, moats, sashes, stockings, candles, and so on. Still other images present rich opportunities for paraphrasing that introduces new words for familiar objects: outfit for clothes, staff for stick, off in the distance for over there, gender for boy or girl, and so on—words they want to know, in part because of curiosity that builds from thinking about what one sees.

Importantly, it's not just the teacher who introduces new vocabulary during VTS discussions. Children also learn from each other. For example, one child recognizes some aspect of an image and uses vocabulary that is new to another when mentioning it, a situation described by Lev Vygotsky, the scholar of early learning: the "more capable peer" models language that a second child hears in use. The teacher repeats it in a paraphrase and points to what is mentioned in the image. A context for learning new language is created.

Classroom practice has indicated that this is particularly helpful to children whose home language is something other than English. What teachers have reported is that second language learners in second grade, who might not always speak up during discussions, reveal that they've taken in the language when asked to write following image discussions.

The most important way to prepare for VTS discussions with young children is to preview the images and to think about what you might hear from your students. While the focus as you lead the discussion is on listening to your students, pointing to what they mention, and paraphrasing each child—echoing their thoughts, not yours—it speeds the process if you have thought in advance about what they might notice and mention. This is an activity that can be undertaken collaboratively with other teachers. In any case, if you have vocabulary in mind, it will help you rephrase what you hear. You can also listen for children's later use of those words in conversation.

Of course, words without context are just words, which is one reason we don't recommend strategies such as Word Walls or Word Maps. Rather, using words to think and talk about subjects of interest during authentic communication is the real catalyst for becoming literate. That's where VTS can truly enhance the prepared environment. When children have access to images that are appropriately chosen for their developmental plane, often they will elect to continue discussions beyond the VTS lesson. In those unfacilitated cases, it is not uncommon to see pairs or triads of children sharing not just observations but also stories about either the image itself or associations the image triggers.

Childhood and Adolescence: Conceptual and Social Exploration

For older children, language learning becomes an integrative activity rather than an end in itself. Vocabulary, syntax, and other mechanical elements of spoken and written language are still developing, but by the time children enter the elementary environment, we expect them to be competent users of language—both to receive and to express knowledge. The VTS lesson, like community meeting or even Great Lessons, becomes a weekly ritual of communal exploration and deep meaning-making of very special source material. It's a time to practice intentional listening, increasingly sophisticated interpretation and articulation of ideas, and collaborative processing. It's a time of very rapid and often dramatic growth in thinking and communicating.

Chapter 3: VTS and Language Development

Not all six-year-olds are "fully competent" language users, and this is particularly true of those for whom English is a second language. Here, VTS serves as a subtle, but powerful intervention, offering the child who may be struggling with comprehension of texts the opportunity to participate in a way that capitalizes on strengths while not drawing attention to deficits. They see perfectly well and grasp what they see, and however they express themselves, the teacher's paraphrases make certain that their ideas contribute usefully to discussions. Within the group experience, all children benefit from the practice of looking and thinking, aided by thoughtful paraphrasing, and the expertise of more language-competent peers who model more fluent language use.

As observational capacities grow, the language to express the increasing complexity of what they see follows. Within a very short time, students add descriptive detail to observations, infer more possible meanings, begin to see and describe things in relation to one another, support their observations with evidence, acknowledge the contributions of others, and engage in respectful, lively debate. All of these thinking and social behaviors reveal themselves in students' language, driving vocabulary, syntax, and the complexity of sentences. Growth is first evident during the VTS discussions themselves (Chapter 4 will discuss ways to track that growth), but when VTS plays a central role in the social and intellectual life of a classroom, that growth can extend well beyond periodic image discussions.

Following VTS discussions, practitioners of VTS in elementary programs often give students the opportunity to write about images. The prompt can be very simple: Write what you think is going on in an image (one they just discussed); make sure you give evidence to back up your ideas. Because of the extended conversations they have just had, students have ideas and words in mind and this makes the task of writing easier than it often is. Having an open-ended time to write allows them additional opportunity to think through the meanings conveyed by an image and sometimes produces new insights.

In any case, writing allows students to operate as individuals. During VTS discussions, students are supported by peer interaction and teacher facilitation: Writing shows what students take away from discussions and retain without such supports. Furthermore, most students appreciate having a visual prompt when asked to write even if they haven't discussed it in advance of writing.

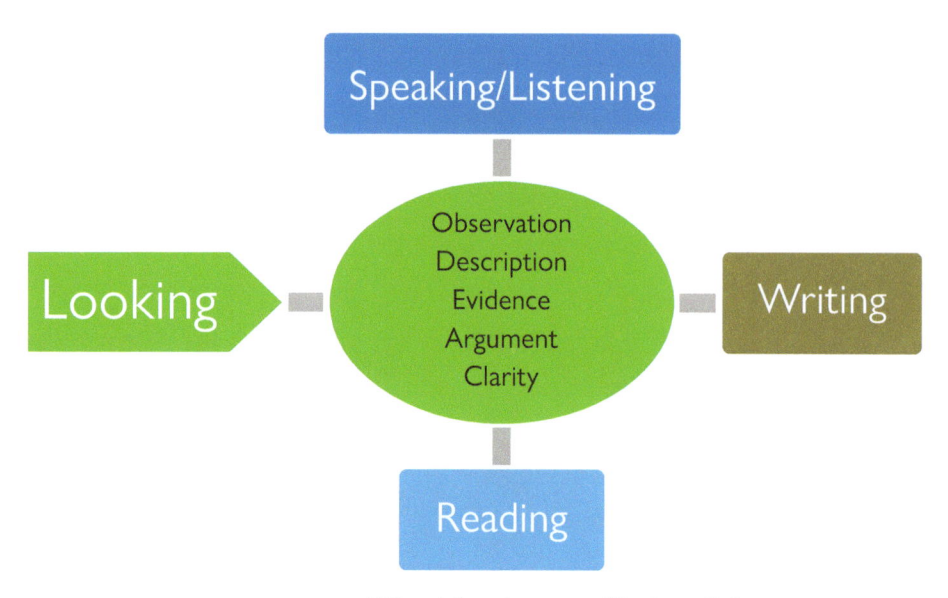

FIGURE 3.1 VTS and Core Language/Thinking Skills

As Figure 3.1 illustrates, the core thinking skills of observation, description, evidence, argument, and clarity are all developed and expressed through ongoing experiences with speaking, listening, and writing. Within this context, looking becomes a catalyzing activity. Visual perception is now one of an array of tools elementary students use to develop critical and creative thinking. Perceiving concepts, sharing perceptions and ideas, revising opinions, and elaborating on observations and inferences are all nurtured by VTS discussions. VTS and the process of careful looking as well as thinking aloud and in writing become integral to ongoing conceptual exploration and growth.

Building on Skills Developed through Looking and Discussing

Weekly VTS discussions are a principal venue in which to practice thinking and communication skills. When the VTS process becomes second nature (and it happens pretty quickly), students can engage in facilitated discussions about other sorts of images in fields as diverse as botany, zoology, geography, history, literature, and math. Teachers who become adept at facilitating VTS discussions often find themselves using the key VTS elements across the curriculum. It's common, for instance, to hear a teacher open a lesson involving an aquarium, a poem, or a math word problem with the question: "What going on here?" followed by "What did you see (or read) that makes you say that?" and of course, "What more can you find?" to keep the discussion going.

When choosing images—and texts—from any discipline, keep certain criteria in mind: Appropriate topics not only contain elements children quickly recognize but also aspects that are up for deliberation—ones that provoke a range of opinions and are debatable, material to chew on, so to speak. You want to encourage students to go beyond what is obvious to them and gain practice at deeper thinking, probing for a variety of and different levels of meaning, practices useful in subjects across disciplines. This practice is core to cosmic education in that it mirrors what disciplinary experts (scientists, mathematicians, historians) do: they make observations and then start to ruminate on the variety of conclusions that might be drawn.

Looking Circles

Once students have learned the basic rigors of VTS discussions, it's appropriate to let them interact with both the pictures and one another in new ways. This is particularly true of upper elementary students and adolescents. One strategy for activating students' natural desire for independence, novelty, and social contact is a variation on the practice of literature circles that some teachers use. The goal is simply to offer another venue in which to engage with the images in ways that catalyze the sharing of meaning.

In order for this to work, students need to have become comfortable with the norms of group interaction, which are modeled during the whole-group discussions facilitated by you. Just as important, the analytical and communication skills developed during VTS discussions help ensure that the student-led discussions are robust and substantive.

When you are ready to introduce this small group work, students should be divided into groups of six or seven; you need enough participants to have a rich variety of comments. Assemble the groups with care: They should be composed of students with a range of abilities and styles—some leaders, some followers, some who are confident speakers, and others who are more reticent.

These small-group, student-led discussions allow students both to practice their looking and thinking skills and to play specified roles in managing the group. A volunteer can take on the facilitator role—asking the questions, listening, pointing, paraphrasing—but it can be done by a team of two students working collaboratively too. They can take turns or assume different tasks, one asking the questions and another responding to comments, for example. Someone else might act as a note-taker so that afterwards they have a record of what was discovered.

Each group should have one or more images to discuss, with members assuming the roles they have volunteered to take—and if there are no volunteers, you can assign tasks. Generally, students work with printed reproductions of the images, though they can also work from digital versions on laptops or iPads. Discussions may last between 15 and 25 minutes. You can elect to have groups report out on their discussions or collect their note sheets in a portfolio. Writing afterwards is always an option too.

Building Skills through Writing and Research

Some elementary and adolescent classrooms incorporate a variety of informal writing opportunities such as a journals or daily writing prompts. All students between the ages of six and eighteen engage in more formal writing via regular, student-generated research. Art images, particularly those that have been discussed in a VTS lesson, can be powerful prompts for both informal and formal writing activities.

Informal Writing

Experts on the writing process have long argued that writers only become better through lots of practice putting pen to paper. In the 1970s, Peter Elbow coined the term "freewriting" and urged all would-be writers to establish writing as a habit—a way of activating the thinking/writing muscle so that ideas flow more easily from the mind to the page. Sometimes known as "prewriting" or "writing to learn," the central tenet of this type of work is that it is informal, which is to say ungraded and often private.

Informal writing generates fluency and serves as a seedbed for ideas that might be further developed in more formal essays. The point, in this context, is to jumpstart writing, and VTS experience has shown that when images are used as prompts, the process often becomes easier, even for reluctant writers. This is especially true if students are given a chance to write after discussions as we have mentioned, when they can build on a combination of factors: They have had opportunity to articulate their ideas, teachers have restated their ideas by paraphrasing each comment, and they've heard the language and ideas of their peers. Writing afterwards anchors the language both used and heard, supporting fluency.

WRITING FOLLOWING A VTS DISCUSSION: REFLECTION, ANALYSIS, SYNTHESIS

While the VTS questions are effective to prompt writing, additional questions can extend thinking launched during a VTS discussion. Reflective, analytic, and synthetic prompts give students a chance to articulate the way in which ideas have developed through conversation and collective meaning-making. Here are some examples of prompts you might use following a VTS discussion:

- *Write a story about what the people in this picture are doing: what might have come before and what happens next.*

- *Recall the discussion and focus specifically on a comment made by one of your classmates that made you think differently about the picture. What did that person say and why did it make you think in a new way?*

- *What did you want to say during the discussion that you didn't have a chance to express to the group?*

- *Tell the story of your own thinking during the discussion; what were your beginning ideas about the picture? What were you thinking when the discussion came to an end; and how did your thinking change over the course of the conversation?*

WRITING PRIOR TO OR IN PLACE OF A DISCUSSION

Sometimes writing about images in advance or even instead of discussion is appropriate. Just as with most activities in the prepared environment, writing about images should never be forced or prescribed. Rather, writing should always be a choice, for example, as independent exploration during a work period. To foster this option, you can create a basket of writing prompt "slips" to be used with a collection of 8x10 reproductions, housed in a notebook or folder. Students may choose one or two to write about. As mentioned earlier, rephrasing the basic VTS questions works to initiate writing, asking, for example, "What's going on in this picture? Remember to provide visual evidence to back up your ideas. And keep looking for more details to add." However, different questions may also invite other kinds of exploration. For example:

- *What does this image make you wonder about?*

- *Write a poem in which you describe this image.*

- *Does this picture remind you of another image you may have seen? How? What do you see that looks similar? What do you see that looks different?*

In some instances, giving students a chance to gather their thoughts before writing can be helpful. Options include:

- *Look carefully at this picture before you start to write. Make notes about what attracts your attention most. Perhaps you can complete this sentence: "When I look at this picture, the first thought that comes into my head is_____."*

- *Make further notes about the central action, the various characters, the setting, the time depicted. Think about the evidence you'll provide to back up your ideas as you write about what's happening in this image.*

Research and Other Formal Writing

Images and VTS image discussions can inspire formal discursive writing, such as personal essays, research reports, or concept papers. In these cases, journal entries or responses to writing prompts can be the seeds for writing that, through reflection, moves from fragment, idea, or question into a fully crafted piece of writing to share with an audience.

In Montessori environments, exploration is often framed as research. Such projects vary from a quick survey conducted to answer a very specific question (What is it about this kind of picture that interests you?) to extended, independent investigations (Read about the early years of an author or painter you like. How might experiences in childhood have shown up in his or her work?). In the best cases, these projects are the result of student choice. Something in the child's life triggers an interest—a trip to a city, the birth or going off to college of a sibling, a summer job, the death of a grandparent, a love of peanut butter or chocolate or tea, a visit to a museum. Almost any authentic interest can be turned into a research question, perhaps with your help.

Sometimes children become fascinated with questions surrounding pictures: the historical setting, the tools key figures may be manipulating, the issues they may be discussing, and for older students, the artist him- or herself. If students decide to engage in image-inspired research, the bulk of that investigation may take place out of the classroom. However, if you help them with online research or draw their attention to resources in your classroom library, you can feed continued enthusiasm. Likewise, if the image or artist chosen is represented in a local art museum, this can become an authentic reason for either a field trip or a going out.

Further Reading

Smith, A. (1966). *Communication and Culture: Readings in the Codes of Human Interaction.* New York: Holt, Rinehart & Winston.

Tomasello, M. (2003a). *Constructing a language.* Cambridge: Harvard University Press.

Tomasello, M. (2003b). The key is social cognition. In D. Gentner & S. Kuczaj (Eds.), *Language and thought* (pp. 47–58). Cambridge, MA: MIT Press.
Tomasello, M., Kruger, A. C., & Ratner, H. H. (1993). Cultural learning. *Behavioral and Brain Sciences*, 16, 495-552.

Elbow, P. (1998). *Writing Without Teachers. 2nd Edition.* New York: Oxford University Press.

Elbow, P. (1998). *Writing with Power: Techniques for Mastering the Writing Process. 2nd Edition.* New York: Oxford University Press.

Emig, J. (1968). *The Composing Processes of Twelfth Graders.* Urbana: National Council of Teachers of English.

Mercer, N. (2000). *Words and Minds: How We Use Language to Think Together.* London: Routledge.

Mercer, N. (2019). *Language and the Joint Creation of Knowledge: The Selected Works of Neil Mercer.* London: Routledge.

Ong, W.J. (2002). *Orality and Literacy.* London: Routledge.

Purcell-Gates, V. (1997). *Other People's Words: The Cycle of Low Literacy.* Cambridge: Harvard University Press.

Resnick, L. and Snow, C. (2009). *Speaking and Listening for Preschool Through Third Grade.* Pittsburgh: University of Pittsburgh Press and The National Center on Education and the Economy.

CHAPTER 4

VTS and Assessment

VTS nurtures a variety of behaviors in several domains: cognitive, linguistic, and social. Some of these are most easily seen during discussions, others tracked by way of writing, and some noticeable in other situations including playtime. Several tools help us detect growth in both thinking and communication, growth we can count on to bolster learning in a variety of arenas. The goal of the tools described in this chapter is to enable teachers to make both observation and reflection ongoing and systematic. In this way, VTS can offer powerful enrichment for core elements of Montessori pedagogy.

One way to activate the observation muscle as we watch our students work is to ask: "What's going on?" It's a deceptively simple question and obviously a direct reference to the VTS starting question. Just as it inspires multidimensional consideration of what's happening within a picture, the question stimulates powerful consideration of the circumstances of learning. We think this question is the most important driver of genuine assessment. Although there are ways to quantify VTS-nurtured change, reflecting on what we see as teachers is most important.

The other two VTS questions are also useful in guiding this effort. We need evidence to back up conclusions we draw—"What we have seen that makes us think…"—and we must keep thinking about "What more can we find?" to ensure that our assessments are rich, accurate, and serve our students well. What we come to understand about individuals, about how children connect to us and to each other, and about how they behave in concert all devolves from observations we make and then think about, ideally discussing them with our peers.

Like Montessori, reflection is baked deep into VTS pedagogy. Pulling back to think about what a child says in order to paraphrase is the first step in reflecting on behavior. Each comment provides data that illuminate both thinking (what interests a child as well as what they think about the things they notice) and language capability at a precise moment (how they express their thoughts). Each successive comment adds to what we know and the material we have to reflect on to assess changes. When we listen intently to accurately grasp a child's thoughts, and as we consider how to rephrase the comment, we are briefly seeing and thinking as the child does. We are following the child.

Remembering later what each child said in fast-moving discussions is challenging but reflecting as soon as possible afterwards—ideally while looking at the pictures discussed to remind you of what was mentioned—allows you to build a cumulative register of behavior. At any one moment, you can focus on one or a few students you are particularly interested in understanding better. Over time, you amass good data with substantiating evidence to share with others, including parents and sometimes with children directly.

Chapter 4: VTS and Assessment

Looking, Thinking, and Talking... and Growing

In young children, for whom spoken language is emerging rapidly, VTS can illuminate the types of talk children tend to favor. As discussed in Chapter 3, very young children tend initially to engage in VTS discussions by naming objects or figures they observe. As their experience exploring images with peers increases and as their language skills generally deepen, we usually notice growth toward more detailed observation. A "girl," for instance, becomes a "little girl." It's not difficult to hear this kind of change. These language changes come as a result of shifts in thinking, from single observations to seeing detail and context. Sentences result from children making inferences based their observations and are most frequently associated with finding very short narratives in the depiction, usually descriptions of an action: "She's eating her breakfast," for example.

Similar patterns may also be observed in older students, particularly those who normally have difficulty engaging through either spoken or written language. Straightforward observations increase in number, become more detailed, and often include context: "There's a building" becomes "There's a building and I think it's a factory and it's in an old part of town." The student infers the function of the building and where it is from what he sees; numbers of such inferences increase and each requires more language to convey. When supplying evidence, the sentences become more complex: "I think it's a factory because it doesn't have any windows."

These shifts are the results of the impact of VTS on thinking. They can be grouped into two categories, one focusing on visual literacy and the other on skills that are key aspects of critical thinking in general.

This is what we mean by visual literacy:

- Making observations: from few to many; from simple—maybe one word—to detailed; from single elements to things in combinations and in context

- Inferring meaning from those observations; also, more over time

- Providing evidence to back up inferences

- Probing for more ideas: staying with inquiry for longer
- Tolerating ambiguity: comfort with more than one possible meaning

This is what we mean by critical thinking, some skills overlapping with visual literacy:

- Collaborative problem solving: Listening to peers who also contribute observations and information; considering what others contribute; discussing and debating with civility; scaffolding; the group out-achieving what any individual can do: "group mind"
- Habitually providing evidence to back up ideas in different contexts
- Considering multiple points of view: holding a variety of views as plausible
- Speculating among alternative inferences: it could be this or it could be that
- Willingness to debate possibilities with others: understanding the value of group process
- Elaborating: returning to add detail, new ideas
- Revising: returning to an earlier point because of a change of mind

We make the categorical differences because we think that understanding and nurturing visual literacy address the values of Montessori educators particularly. Moreover, today's world is so full of images that being able to decode them quickly and accurately is crucial.

The same may be said about critical thinking. Most of the challenges we face as a world are enormous, complex, and multifaceted—more gray than black and white. Ditto the solutions. The work that lies ahead of students we educate today requires flexible, reflective, imaginative thinkers with the capacity to collaborate, persevere, question, rethink, revise, and resolve.

Of course, Montessori educators have always been committed to preparing children for the real world. The basic elements of VTS support that preparation. The behaviors listed above, identified through collecting data over more than a dozen years in a series of studies, don't happen all at once, nor are they the result of VTS alone.

Still, these outcomes will be reliably in place by the end of the elementary years if VTS is regularly incorporated into your teaching practice.

Measuring Thinking

Critical, creative, and interpretive skills manifest themselves verbally, in oral and written expression. Data have shown them to appear in all students, though not necessarily to the same degree, and it's often the students who struggle in other lessons who show the fastest growth, rising to norms and above. The teacher's facilitation skills impact the amount of change as does their willingness to apply VTS in other lessons. The more discussions students have, the more the thinking behaviors become habitual, and the greater their related impact on language.

What Growth Looks Like: Applying VTS Research Methodology

Several strategies can support keeping track of this developmental arc, including making notes after discussions. While the original VTS research relied heavily on open-ended interviews, today the most common way we measure thinking is by analyzing writing. Below we provide tools for assessing discussions as well as writing samples. First, however, we want to provide some orientation to what counts as evidence of growth.

VTS researchers have been trained to code oral and written responses to works of art based on a manual developed by VTS co-founder Housen. The first step of coding an interview or writing sample is sometimes called "parsing"—the process of identifying units of thought as they are expressed by the viewer so that they can be analyzed. Like the process of recording and analyzing Montessori "work curves," this process is laborious and time consuming. Yet the depth of this analysis provides rich insight into what is going on with children as they develop critical thinking and visual literacy. We think it's useful to spend some time on what the process entails and what is learned from it.

Two moves anchor the process. If you have a sample of student writing about an image (and we discuss how to get such samples later in this chapter), the first step in analyzing it is to parse it, breaking it into units that can be studied. For example, in this comment there are two different observations in one sentence; we consider them two thought units and insert double slash marks—//—between the two:

In front of the image, there is a woman's head, // then a woman covering some of her head with a small person.

Once you have broken the sample into thought units, you can take the second step and consider what kind of thinking each unit exhibits. In the sample above, you have two "detailed observations."

Borrowing from Housen and her colleagues while studying the impact of VTS, six traits describe the most common thinking expressed both orally during discussions and in writing. They are:

- Simple observations—naming; a single word, listing, or labeling

- Detailed observations—includes adjectives and language that locates the observation

- Drawing inferences from observations without providing evidence to back them up—conclusions drawn from observations; the building blocks of narratives

- Supported observations or inferences—conclusions drawn from observations backed up by evidence, a foundational element of critical thinking

- Speculating—enumerating multiple possible inferences, often using conditional or qualifying language

- Elaboration—adding detail to an earlier thought

Just as becoming familiar with child behavior that indicates various levels of concentration is essential to your Montessori training, recognizing these thinking traits contributes to your understandings of cognition. Practice looking for them in children's talk and writing. Once they become second nature to you, you will notice them everywhere.

Chapter 4: VTS and Assessment

Abstracting the Method: Tools for Assessing Discussion and Writing

The tools described here depend on your recognizing the traits listed above—recognizing the difference between simple observations and detailed observations, for example, and knowing when a child is inferring meaning or noticing when they give evidence. The behaviors become familiar to you as you paraphrase their comments.

To help you keep track of growth, it always makes sense to study only a few students at any one time, perhaps choosing ones you want to understand better. Over time, you can accumulate data about more and more students.

We offer two rubrics that can be used for analyzing discussions. The first is for use with younger students and older students when VTS is first introduced. The second is for older students later in the process. Both tools focus on listening to and observing students' behavior: continuously asking "what's going on?" to enable to better understand each child's growth trajectory.

Behaviors can be tracked at the time of the discussion if you have an assistant teacher who is familiar with the thinking behaviors described—knowing what a detailed observation is and how it differs from naming, for example. When you are working by yourself, and have no one to observe a lesson, fill out the rubrics below based on your memory of what happened during the discussion. Of course, the more quickly you sit down to fill out the form, the more likely you are to accurately recall what you heard among the few students you chose to focus on. Looking at the image as you reconstruct the discussion usually helps jog your memory too.

The rubric on the next page (Figure 4.1) pinpoints behaviors found in various studies to be the earliest to occur. Because of the connection between thinking and language, we include space in this rubric to make notes about expressive fluency of each student. Each instance of a behavior is marked with a forward slash.

Chapter 4: VTS and Assessment

STUDENT	SIMPLE OBSERVATIONS/ NAMING	DETAILED/PINPOINTED OBSERVATIONS	INFERENCES	EVIDENCE	SPEECH MECHANICS ARTICULATION, FLUENCY, VOCABULARY
Sammy L.	////	///	//	/	Sammy's language ability is above average especially in terms of vocabulary.
Marielle J.	//				M is a non-native English speaker and struggles to articulate her ideas.
Charlie P.	//// //	//// //			C excels at noticing fine detail; tends to speak in clipped phrases rather than sentences. Sometimes stammers.

FIGURE 4.1 Excerpt from Sample Tracking Form I: Types of Talk

The students listed here represent a sample from a lower elementary class in a public Montessori school. Each has demonstrated difficulty during regular class discussions of texts and other topics, and all three are part of the school's Child Study program. That means they are receiving classroom-based interventions to support language challenges. The sample was taken early in the semester, after only two lessons with VTS.

Sammy, who is often disruptive during work periods, is fully engaged in VTS discussions and shows evidence of not only high-level participation but also the ability to both articulate his ideas in narrative form and provide precise, detailed observations of the pictures discussed.

Marielle, by contrast, is hampered by her basic language difficulties and is only able to name objects she notices in the pictures. Still she participates; she's usually reticent in other lessons. Teachers think that pointing and paraphrasing give Marielle needed support because she sees that the teacher is following her thoughts and hears them provide the vocabulary she wants, anchored in a visual.

Charlie speaks often and, like Sammy, is able to observe and articulate fine details, but he lacks fluency. His teachers will pay special attention as they rephrase his comments, trying to model the fluency he needs. They will look more closely at his participation over the next four to six weeks. If significant improvement is not evident at that point, Charlie may benefit from more clinical consideration of speech challenges.

If you have a teaching assistant to collect the data as each discussion unfolds, then reflect together as you fill in the qualitative commentary. All data are pertinent as you discuss "what's going on?" with your peers and can be used as both a diagnostic and an intervention for child study. Over time, it can also be used to scan the entire group and provide you with more generalized insight into patterns evident across all students.

The second rubric, below (Figure 4.2) is a tool to be used with students who have had more experience and are most likely in upper elementary or higher. The range of thinking behaviors highlighted are those commonly demonstrated by students after eight to ten discussions. As you reflect on what you have seen and annotated with your peers, you may want to replace or add behaviors to this array mentioning, for example, aspects of participation, interactions, and language fluency.

STUDENT	PINPOINTED OBSERVATIONS	INFERENCES	EVIDENCE W/ PROMPT	EVIDENCE W/ OUT PROMPT	SPECULATION	INCORPORATING OBSERVATIONS OF OTHERS	SPEECH MECHANICS
Sally	///	//	/////		//	/	
Ricardo	////		///	////	/	///	
Lin	////-///	///	////	///	//		

FIGURE 4.2 Excerpt from Sample Tracking Form 2: Types of Thought

While any one of the behaviors can occur at any time during the school year, behaviors such as supplying evidence without prompt and revision tend to emerge after substantial experience with VTS. The sample noted in the rubric above was taken after about five VTS lessons; no notes were taken about speech mechanics. While all students were able to provide evidence when prompted by the question "What do you see that makes you say that?" Ricardo and Lin were also able to support their observations with evidence spontaneously. Only Ricardo consistently incorporated the observations of others, making him the outlier at this point. His example is likely to assist the skill development of others. It is not surprising to find this range of behaviors including the discrepancies after relatively few lessons.

Like the beginner tool, this one may be used to target specific students you want to understand better. It can be used with additional students over time and, like the beginner tool, it can eventually be helpful in seeing whole-group trends. Like all the tools in the chapter, its purpose is to gain a describable sense of what's going on with thinking and communicating among your students. When you notice students like Lin and Ricardo supply evidence without a prompt during VTS, for example, that is a cue to look for other instances beyond the VTS discussions. It is an invitation to delve more deeply into the concept of evidence with those children and to offer work that will stretch their thinking in that vein. It can also inspire you to use "What do you see that makes you say that?" in other lessons to support building the habit of evidential reasoning in all students; it's obviously a behavior that is within reach.

As with younger children, speech behaviors are correlated with critical thinking. Their syntax often improves and the vocabulary they use expands as students express more complicated thoughts, especially if the teacher has consistently paraphrased providing vocabulary sought by students and well-crafted rephrasing.

Pre- and Post-Writing Samples

While you will notice behavioral change during VTS discussions as well as during other classroom exchanges, the most common form of assessing growth in thought over time is through studying writing samples. This is a staple of VTS methodology. We recommend, at a minimum, collecting and analyzing writing prompts at the start and end of each academic year—a "pre-test" and "post-test," one taken before a set of VTS discussions and a second after six to eight of them.

A sample is given below, but the general instructions include using the same picture for both pre- and post-test to enable direct comparisons. Provide the picture you've chosen for the students to write about—it could be copied on paper with a form on which they can record their thoughts. Or it could be projected for a class to see or provided online. Assign the image a number so you can identify it later for the post-test.

Writing Sample Instructions

Student's name: _____ Date: _____

Teacher's name: _____ Image number: _____

Look closely at this picture. Think about what you see.

Ask yourself: What's going on in this picture? Write down your thoughts. Include as much detail as you notice. Give reasons to back up your ideas.

You have as long as you want to write. Use the back side of this sheet if you need it. Read over your comments before you finish.

_____
_____
_____
_____
_____
_____
_____
_____
_____
_____
_____
_____

Writing Examples Discussed

You can consider such writing samples concrete evidence of a child's thinking, her fluency with language, and the interplay between thinking and language she uses to express increasingly complex ideas. Once you have a pre- and post-test, you can review and compare the writing to determine change over time. You can use the categories in the rubric (Figure 4.2) to guide your analyses of students' thinking.

We'll start off by looking at a pre-test sample. In the comment below from a 6th grade student at a high-needs school, we've inserted double slash marks between distinct thoughts. In this case, each thought corresponds to a sentence. You can't separate phrases within the comment; none would make sense alone.

Chapter 4: VTS and Assessment

PRE-WRITING SAMPLE: GRADE 6

In the image shown, it looks like a woman is using a knife to cut a birthday cake for a little kid on a table w/ candle. // A man behind the woman must be her butler because he is standing straight toward the woman & the kid. // The [kid] looks like he is about to turn 6 years old. //

The first thought is an extended set of five detailed observations (a woman, a knife, a cake, a little kid, a table with candles) with three inferences (using a knife, it's a birthday cake, and it's for the little kid). It's one thought because it would make no sense if you split it into component observations. No evidence is given to back up the inferences: for example, to explain how the student infers the woman is cutting a cake, or why it's a birthday cake, or that it's for the kid. In terms of writing fluency, the sentence is a short introduction to the narrative the student sees unfolding in the image.

The second thought adds further detail, addressing the man who the student observes in detail: he's behind the woman, standing straight. Another inference is drawn from these observations: he must be her butler; this time the student supplies evidence: because of where and how he's standing. The "must be" phrasing is declarative rather than speculative. The latter would have been indicated by use of conditional language: he "might be" a butler.

The third thought is an inference elaborating on the earlier observation about the child: the kid is "about to turn 6 years old." No evidence is provided.

Here is another example which includes the post-test response. We decided that the thought units once again corresponded to complete sentences.

Chapter 4: VTS and Assessment

PABLO PICASSO. FAMILY OF SALTIMBANQUES, 1905. NATIONAL GALLERY OF ART

STUDENT RESPONSE	ANALYSIS OF THOUGHT
Pre-test	**Pre-test**
I see clouds in the sky. //	*Observation (clouds) with detail (in sky)*
I see a lady sitting and staring. //	*Observation (lady) with inference (staring)*
I see a little girl carrying some flowers. //	*Detailed observation (little girl, carrying flowers)*
I see a little boy. //	*Detailed observation (little boy)*
I think I see Santa. //	*Inference with qualification (Santa, I think…)*
I see another boy carrying a bucket. //	*Detailed observation (another boy…)*
Post-test	**Post-test**
I think the girl in the hat is probably posing to take a picture. //	*Detailed observation (girl, hat), qualifications (I think, probably), inference (posing)*
I see a little girl holding a basket full of pink, white flowers. //	*Detailed observation (little girl, etc.)*
I also see a little boy dressed as he was in [karate?]. //	*Detailed observation (little boy) with inference (karate)*
Since people are dressed up in different things it might be Halloween. //	*Speculation among three explanations for "what's going on?" (Halloween, Christmas, wedding) each supported by evidence*
I think it is Christmas because I see a man dressed like Santa Claus and the people are dressed very nice. //	
Maybe somebody is getting married because I see a little girl holding a basket full of flowers. //	

From the pre-test, you know the child can narrate a story grounded in his or her internal logic, based on their experience rather than in evidence derived from the picture. The second sample taken five months later—the post-test—gives you more evidence about how this child thinks and writes—and how certain skills (such as providing evidence or speculating among possibilities) have manifested.

We have parsed the thoughts in one column and indicated the thought categories where we think they belong in the other. The pre-test shows that the student is observant and can provide descriptive detail—the clouds are "in the sky," the little girl is "carrying some flowers," the little boy carries "a bucket." She infers that the woman "is staring" though she doesn't tell us what she sees as evidence of this. She qualifies one observation: "I think I see Santa." She's not certain, but again no evidence is provided. Overall, she gives us a description of what she recognizes. It's basically a list with only two inferences pulled from her observations—the thought that the woman is sitting and staring, and that one character might be Santa.

In the post-test, we have a good deal of evidence of advancing skills. The student is as observant as ever, though she includes more detail in her descriptions and adds the element of possibility to her inferences: the girl is "probably posing to take a picture." Recognition that what she thinks is only a possibility continues in the other conclusions she posits: the outfits "might" indicate that the various characters are dressed for Halloween. Or on the other hand, it's Christmas because of the red outfit on one and the fact that all are dressed "nice." And as a third speculation, maybe someone is getting married. All three interpretations are backed up with evidence. She has concocted three possible scenarios to explain this grouping of people.

Taken together, this detailed process of coding writing samples takes thoughtful and time-consuming effort, but we think the evidence it shows of a child's abilities as well as change make it worth it. We hope you will try it, if not with all your students, with a sample, as a way of familiarizing yourself with the key VTS-nurtured cognitive changes. Doing so will make use of the tools described below more intuitive and more sustainable.

Assessing Writing

The journey from thinking to talking to writing is not linear, but it is progressive, and we know that stronger oral language skills have a positive impact on formal literacy performance. In other words, fluent and nuanced speaking can result in fluent writing. While growth in thinking and speaking reliably show up in the context of VTS discussions first, it's not easy to capture what's going on as you facilitate. Discussions are ephemeral but writing is not and as such can be saved and studied. Their writing about images can provide concrete insight into student performance.

As pointed out above, almost all the writing associated with VTS is informal in nature. Therefore, it's important to be clear that the means of collecting evidence and the evidence itself are limited in their capacity to capture how students fare in their mastery of the craft of writing in general. Rather, what these tools show is *how students represent their thinking on paper in an unpressured, authentic way*. Furthermore, being this attentive to a child's thinking, you have information to factor into your other means of assessing writing: specifically, the interrelationship of thinking to their gradual language development.

WINSLOW HOMER. SNAP THE WHIP, 1872.

For more formal rating, we link tally marks to standards, link thinking behaviors with writing behaviors, and invite the teacher to consider a variety of writing samples—formal as well as informal—in a holistic manner that assumes that thinking and writing are reciprocal endeavors. The following comments were taken from a variety of writing samples about the Winslow image.

	TALLY	BELOW	MEETS	EXCEEDS	ADDITIONAL COMMENTS
Offers observations of the image "There are boys."		(0–3)	(3–5)	(<5)	
Provides detailed observations from the image "Two boys, one wears a red shirt, the other no shoes."		(0–2)	(2–5)	(<5)	
Offers an interpretation "The boys are playing a game."		(0–1)	(1–3)	(<3)	
Supplies evidence to support the interpretation "It looks like a game of chase because the boy in red is running, while the others run after him."		(0–3)	(3–5)	(<5)	
Makes a personal connection or association "It reminds me of my cousins and the games we play."		(0–1)	(1–4)	(<4)	
Expresses multiple possible interpretations/acknowledges multiple points of view "While it looks like a game, it could also be a real chase, where the boy in front has made the others angry."		(0–1)	(1–3)	(<3)	
Poses probing questions "The one boy whose face I can see isn't smiling, and the sky is grey with lots of dark clouds. It makes me wonder if these kids are really having fun."		(0–1)	(1–3)	(<3)	
Expresses points and evidence clearly, using appropriately descriptive vocabulary (as modeled in prior VTS discussions and writing)		(0–4)	(4–6)	(<6)	

FIGURE 4.3 Writing Rubric Excerpt

The rubric above blends key thinking moves such as observation, interpretation, supplying evidence, and speculation with other elements of effective writing, such as making personal associations, posing probing questions, and using language effectively to articulate both opinions and evidence. It is also designed to support nonfiction, expository writing. To adjust this to support work in creative writing, you can add an indicator related to narrative.

An individual student may excel at some of these elements and fall below standard on others. As with all the tools presented in this book, the point is not to use this tool to sort students, but rather to gain a more nuanced understanding of them. For this reason, we don't recommend using this for summative evaluation. Rather, in addition to illuminating what's going on with individual children in terms of thinking and writing, it can provide guidance for teachers as they coach students through drafts.

If this and the other rubrics cited here become useful tools to you, you can share them with students to provide them with the same insights you're gathering. As you explain how you use the tool and what you learn from it, you can supply students with processes for self-evaluation. These in turn give students more agency in their growth and a greater appreciation of their strengths as well as areas ripe for development.

Counting What Counts

The kind of development catalyzed and made visible in VTS is important, and we believe it should become part of standard reporting protocols. The fact that art works are a core part of VTS and are one reason for the growth you can track relates particularly well to key Montessori values. Like executive functions, linguistic and cultural fluency, and social and emotional development, aesthetic development is core to the prospect of human flourishing. The progress reporting template that follows integrates all these behaviors.

Elementary Progress Report
Social, Emotional & Executive Development

Student's Name: _____ D.O.B. _____
Teacher's Name: _____
Term: _____ Absent: _____ Tardy: _____

KEY: **F** = Frequently **O** = Occasionally **R** = Rarely

SOCIAL FLUENCY & EMOTIONAL FLEXIBILITY	MID	END		MID	END
Shows gratitude			Manages frustration and conflict with flexibility		
Accepts responsibility for actions			Interacts appropriately with adults		
Speaks and listens with understanding and respect			Contributes as a community member		
Interacts cooperatively with peers			Maintains healthy habits		
Shows sensitivity to the needs and feelings of others			Models integrity; is truthful in actions and words		
EXECUTIVE FUNCTIONS	**MID**	**END**		**MID**	**END**
Demonstrates initiative			Uses time effectively		
Makes appropriate work choices			Manages impulses		
Sustains appropriate focus during work			Follows multi-step directions		
Persists and follows work through to completion			Seeks help when needed		
Transitions between activities smoothly			Embraces and pursues challenges		
CRITICAL & CREATIVE THINKING	**MID**	**END**		**MID**	**END**
Tolerates uncertainty			Challenges assumptions		
Uses reflection/feedback as a tool for growth			Shows concern for quality of work		
Investigates/Explores interests with passion			Makes conceptual, experiential connections		
Provides detailed observations & descriptions			Supplies evidence for arguments		

COMMENTS:
MID:

FIGURE 4.4 Progress Report Excerpt

In the excerpt above, drawn from the *NCMPS Elementary Developmental Progress Report*, what we list as critical and creative thinking behaviors mark aesthetic development as well. Several of the items directly mirror the tools earlier in this chapter. Others assume that VTS-inspired behavior will show up in other classroom-based activities. The point is that these skills matter. To report on this growth, however, you need ongoing and reliable means of tracking it. We recommend collecting and analyzing data using multiple tools at least three times a year. Moreover, when meeting with families to discuss progress in this area, it can be helpful to share writing samples and examples of demonstrable growth.

Further Reading

National Center for Montessori in the Public Sector. (2019). *The Montessori Assessment Playbook*. Washington, DC: National Center for Montessori in the Public Sector Press.

CHAPTER 5

Further Reflections

We conclude with some reflections on the congruences between VTS and Montessori. We hope, by now, many of them are obvious: the shared conviction that art is a fundamental human endeavor, that looking stimulates all kinds of thinking, that group discussions further develop thinking, and that critical and creative thinking can be nurtured. Furthermore, we hope the connections between thinking and language have been made clear, and how the addition of new thinking behaviors have an impact on a child's language fluency. And we hope as you experiment with VTS, you'll note the impact on social behaviors we all seek. We hope this book stimulates your own exploration of the many ways in which VTS can enrich the prepared environment.

Chapter 5: Further Reflections

Cosmic Education, Human Potential, and Aesthetic Development

Most of the Montessori practitioners we've worked with over the years see an immediate link between what goes on in a Montessori classroom and VTS. They are drawn to opportunities for meaningful group work, deep discussion, and analysis demonstrated by even very young children, and the opportunity to integrate art in ways that go beyond art appreciation. Primary teachers appreciate links between VTS, sense training, and language development. Elementary teachers see VTS as a hook for interdisciplinary, student-driven inquiry. And if it were to stop there, classrooms would be greatly enriched by the inclusion of VTS.

But there is another area we've not touched on that has strong resonance in Montessori classrooms: the social benefits of VTS. Since the early days of VTS research—and throughout the almost thirty years since—teachers have remarked on how their students behave during VTS discussions. For example, even usually reticent children volunteer ideas enthusiastically. And student disagreements cause no discord or rancor, a very positive difference in the view of most. Social and emotional implications of VTS have never been studied in the ways that thinking and impact on language have, but teachers consistently report increases in self-confidence and cooperative interactions, both of these sought and appreciated by Montessori educators and both hard to teach.

The skill of listening is also very hard to teach. So too is the habit of working well with others. VTS discussions assist with teaching both. Careful listening is modeled by teachers, the proof being skillful paraphrases. Equally important, when students are engaged by an intriguing topic and hear many varied responses from peers to that topic, little by little the main purpose of listening becomes clear: you learn good stuff. You have the opportunity to share your views and be introduced to those of others. As students express and debate ideas and consider a range of possible implications of the topics they explore, they are engaging in a collaborative process little different from what experts do in real world explorations of meaty topics. As students participate in VTS discussions—of art and other subjects as well—they come to understand small group work, both how to lead and how to participate in a group process that folds individual uniqueness into a collaborative whole.

Chapter 5: Further Reflections

The links between VTS and Montessori, however, run even deeper. Just as art is a fundamental human need, aesthetic development is central to the fundamental purpose of Montessori education: to appreciate both the order and the challenges of a vast universe; to live intentionally, equipped to confront and resolve problems, conflicts, and puzzles of all kinds; and to discern one's contribution to society. Aesthetic development mirrors the goals of Montessori education and provides access to skills for both children and teachers.

For students, the development of aesthetic thinking through VTS offers access to ways of making sense of all they discover in the world. It makes use of cognitive processes that begin in infancy, are well honed by early childhood, and are often overlooked afterwards. Like the sense training that sets the stage for abstract and creative thinking, VTS trains the mind to consider thoughts and feelings, to explore possibilities, to entertain multiple points of view, to build knowledge in community.

As children mature, VTS brings students into direct contact with ideas that matter to them. In the process, VTS assists viewers in developing rigorous thinking; finely polished social skills; and a deeper sense of respect, community and trust. Critical thinking, resilience, perseverance, optimism: these are all core values of the Montessori experience. And they are also central to the VTS experience.

For teachers, the fundamental VTS question—*what's going on in this picture?*—offers deep consideration of the fundamental Montessori skill of observation. How do we make sense of what we see in art, text, the environment and, not incidentally, in children? How do we learn to appreciate the secrets of childhood in ways that help us better serve children and families? In short, including practice focused on aesthetic growth makes us better teachers.

Aesthetic thinking can be summarized as the union of thinking and feeling, and as such it is core to the process of understanding who children are and how best to serve them. Indeed, the signal VTS question: "What's going on?" becomes the touchstone for the Montessori teacher seeking to deepen their skills of observation, perception, and analysis. Growing as a viewer of works of art, it turns out, transfers to making sense of all manner of phenomena. We hope that all adults will develop that aesthetic habit of asking "What's going on with this child?" "What's going on with this environment?" "What's going on with this family?" "What's going on with me?"

Imagination Is Grounded in Perception

We don't know if Maria Montessori and Rudolph Arnheim (who coined the term "visual thinking") ever met. Their career trajectories, however, placed them in some of the same physical places and intellectual circles, and their respective orientations toward human flourishing overlapped in ways that suggest they shared a common set of understandings about thinking and imagination. Perhaps most poignant is the shared conviction that imagination is grounded in perception. While Arnheim articulated the integral connection between looking and thinking, Montessori grounded her own educational theory in the importance of all the senses in shaping not just thought, but physical, emotional, and spiritual formation.

Among other things, VTS serves as a powerful rejoinder to the common critique that Montessori fails at encouraging imagination because it discourages fantasy. First, Maria Montessori didn't discourage fantasy. She simply observed that it didn't need to be nurtured. She also observed, like Arnheim and other scholars of aesthetic thought,[2] that imagination blends cognitive and emotional skills and, like other advanced skills, demands cultivation. Executive functions and critical, creative, or imaginative thinking all require ongoing practice. Developing understanding of how, for instance, a shape exists in space (in both two and three dimensions) and how shapes can be combined to form other shapes does not preclude the concoction of a story. Rather, it provides substance for the invention of that story.

Just as important, the cultivation of imagination is developmental. Which is to say, what we do when we are very young sets the stage for what comes after. And the richer the child's perceptual education, the better able they will be to deploy such skills in the interest of invention, speculation, and divergent as well convergent thinking.

It is perfectly clear that we need the adults of the future to be prepared to reimagine and reinvent a world different and better than the one they inherit, a sentiment congruent with the intentions of Maria Montessori. The world she envisioned was more peaceful and kinder than the one she inhabited. In it, children would be taught

---

2 Baldwin, James Mark. *Thought and Things: A Study of the Development and Meaning of Thought or Genetic Logic*. 3 vols. New York: Macmillan, 1906–1911.

in more humane and developmentally sensible ways, nurturing their empathy and concern for one another and their care for the environment around them. They would be empowered to engage with challenges they encounter in thoughtful, imaginative ways.

These children are in our charge today. We hope that including VTS in the intelligent surroundings of the Montessori classroom will help us serve Montessori's vision well.

Acknowledgments

Finishing details of this book were completed with the invaluable assistance of Katie Brown, Director of Professional Learning at the National Center for Montessori in the Public Sector, Keith Whitescarver, who with Jacqueline Cossentino founded the National Center for Montessori in the Public Sector, and with the immeasurable thoughtfulness and enthusiasm of Hillary Murphy.

Printed in the USA
CPSIA information can be obtained
at www.ICGtesting.com
LVHW071058150324
774517LV00028B/984